# THE BEGINNER'S GUIDE TO GUITAR

By Travis John Andrews and Ruth Parry

STRING LETTER PUBLISHING

Publisher: David A. Lusterman
Group Publisher and Editorial Director: Dan Gabel
Education Editor: Dan Apczynski
Director of Design and Production: Barbara Summer
Production Manager: Hugh O'Connor
Print Production: Andy Djohan and Sam Lynch

Cover Photograph: Barbara Summer

ISBN 978-1-890490-69-0

This book was produced by String Letter Publishing, Inc.
PO Box 767, San Anselmo, CA 94979-0767
(415) 485-6946; StringLetter.com

STRING LETTER PUBLISHING

# CONTENTS

# CD TRACK LIST

# INTRODUCTION

Welcome to the *Beginner's Guide to Guitar*! If you're reading this page, then you've taken the first steps toward an enriching lifelong relationship with the guitar. Whether your passions lie in rock, jazz, blues, instrumental fingerstyle, or any other style of music, the lessons in this book will introduce you to easy chords, melodies, and rhythmic patterns you need to begin playing guitar with a solid foundation.

## The Parts of the Guitar

Before you get started with these lessons, it's a good idea to cover a few of the basics. The diagram shown here identifies the different parts of the acoustic and electric guitar, many of which will be referred to throughout this guide. Consult this diagram whenever you need it.

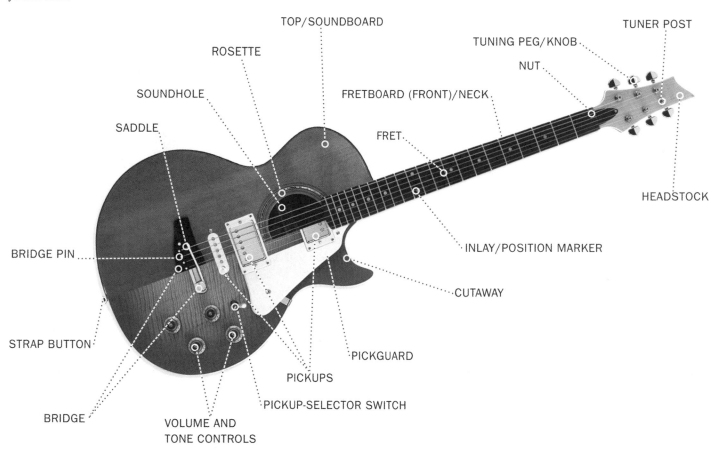

## Holding Your Guitar

Learning how to hold your guitar is very important—the position of your body can have a big impact on your ability to play well.

First, let's clarify a few terms: Your **fretting hand** is the hand that you'll use to press the guitar strings onto the fretboard when playing different notes and chord shapes. For most guitarists this is the left hand (although if you have a "left-handed guitar," your fretting hand would be your right hand). These lessons will focus a great deal on the fingers of the fretting hand, which are usually referred to by number; when we talk about the first, second, third, and fourth fingers, we're referring to the index, middle, ring, and pinky fingers of the fretting hand. Meanwhile, the hand responsible for strumming the strings and picking individual notes is called your **picking hand**.

The two most common postures for guitar playing are often called **classical sitting position** and **casual sitting position**. In classical sitting position, the leg on the fretting-hand side of the body is raised slightly (many players use a small footstool for this, although a hard guitar case or small stack of books can make a handy substitute). The guitar is positioned over the raised knee at an upward angle, so that the body makes contact with the guitar at four points: the inner left and right thighs, the chest, and the picking-hand forearm. In casual sitting position, the guitar is placed over the knee opposite the fretting hand with the neck elevated at a slight angle. In both positions, it's important to try keeping your back and neck straight, with the guitar's top angled very slightly upward offering a glimpse of the fretboard.

If your guitar has strap buttons, you can also use a guitar strap to play from a **standing position**. Secure the strap to your guitar and carefully position it so that the strap comes over the fretting-hand shoulder and under the picking-hand arm. Experiment with different strap lengths to find your comfort zone, but avoid letting the guitar hang so low that it puts your fretting-hand wrist at an odd angle.

As you play, keep your fretting-hand thumb positioned behind the neck, using it as a bracing point for your fretting-hand fingers. Avoid touching the neck with the palm of your fretting hand. The music examples in these lessons are intended to be played in **first position** (in which the fretting-hand fingers stay between the first and fourth frets), so placing the thumb behind the second fret should give you the right amount of support to play anything you'll see here.

Classical sitting position.

## Tuning Your Guitar

In standard tuning, the guitar's six strings are tuned to the pitches E, A, D, G, B, and E, in that order, from the thickest (sixth) string to the thinnest (first) string.

There are different ways to get your guitar in tune. For pitch reference, you can use an electronic tuner, pitch pipe, or tuning fork, any of which can be found at a local music store. You can also tune to the sound of someone else's guitar (if it's already in tune) or to another instrument, like a piano. To change the pitch of a string, gently turn the appropriate tuning peg to tighten or loosen each string: tighten a string to raise its pitch, and loosen a string to lower its pitch. As you experiment with your tuning pegs, be careful not to overtighten any of the strings—they can break if you're not careful. If you're tuning a string by ear to another pitch, listen carefully to the desired note and adjust the tuning peg until the sound of the string matches the sound of the reference pitch. For the best results, tune up to the desired pitch from below.

Once you've successfully tuned your low sixth string to an E note, you can use your own guitar to tune the other strings. Press the sixth string at the fifth fret with your fretting hand and strike the string with your thumb or pick—this should give you an A note. Use that note as a reference pitch to tune your open fifth string. Once it's tuned to A, press the fifth fret of the fifth string and strike the string for a D note, which you can then use to tune your open fourth string. Repeat this process one more time with the fourth string to tune the open third string to G. Press the *fourth* fret of your tuned third string for your next reference pitch, B, and use it to tune the guitar's second string. Finally, press the tuned second string at the fifth fret for an E note, and use that pitch to tune the guitar's high first string. The ability to hear differences in pitch takes a while to develop, so don't be discouraged if this process isn't easy for you right away—the good news is that practice time spent tuning your guitar will help your musical ear develop quickly! The tuning diagram shown here can help walk you through the process as we've described it.

Casual sitting position.

Proper fretting-hand thumb placement.

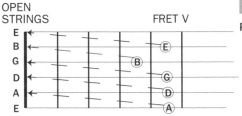

TRACK 1

# LESSON 1

## New Chord: E minor

**E**m
xxx000

Let's play our first chord! A *chord* is a group of two or more notes that are played at the same time. Our E-minor chord (often abbreviated "Em"), has three notes: G on the third string, open; B on the second string, open; and E on the first string, open. An open string is one that you play with your picking hand, but not your fretting hand. Start with your pick on the third string and move it downward through the top three strings using a small flick of your wrist—a movement like you'd use to flick some lint off your sweater vest. This is called a *downstroke*. Let the motion come from your wrist (not your elbow), moving the pick across the surface of the strings without digging in too deep. If you get it right, the first, second, and third strings should ring out together, making an Em chord.

### How to Read a Chord Diagram

While looking at this book at your desk or music stand, hold the guitar upright with the headstock pointed at the ceiling and the strings facing you. Each of the vertical lines in the chord diagram's grid represents a string on your guitar. Guitarists often refer to these strings by number—from six (the thickest string) to one (the thinnest) as you look at the guitar from left to right. The horizontal lines in the diagram represent the frets, the metal bars that cross the fretboard. A zero or "O" above a string means to play that string open, by strumming it without placing any fingers on the string. An "X" above a string tells you not to play that string, either because the pitch doesn't belong to a given chord or because you don't need it. Black dots on a chord diagram (although there are none in this Em voicing) indicate where on the fretboard to place your fretting-hand fingers. Typically, each black dot will be accompanied by a number 1–4 above the string, telling you which corresponding finger of your fretting hand is the best choice to fret the designated pitch.

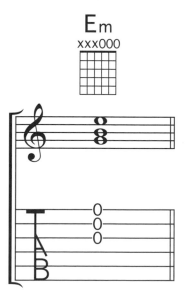

Fretting position for an E-minor chord.

**E**m
xxx000

# Notes on the First String

### E, F, and G (mi, fa, sol)

Let's play our first single notes. Every note has two parts: one is its pitch, identified by a letter name from A to G, and the other is its rhythmic value or duration, counted by beats. In this section, we'll learn three different pitches on the first string of the guitar, after which we'll play around with their rhythmic values.

### Introducing E

The top space on the treble clef staff is where the note E lives. On the guitar, this note can be found on the open first string. In order to play an open string, your fretting hand doesn't need to do anything at all—simply strike the first string with your guitar pick to hear its pitch. The solfége syllable for this note is "mi" (pronounced "me"). Sing the syllable "mi" and try to match the pitch of your voice to the sound of the E note on the guitar.

### Introducing F

A note on the top line of the staff is called F. Using the first finger of your fretting hand, press down the first string at the first fret. With the picking hand, strike the first string to hear how it sounds. Notice that F sounds higher than E—this may be more obvious when you sing it. The solfége syllable for F is "fa" (pronounced "fah"). Use this syllable when you sing the note F.

### Introducing G

The next note sits above the staff and it's called G. Use the third finger of your fretting hand to press down the first string at the third fret. Your index and middle fingers can just hang loose, while keeping close to the fingerboard. Again, with the picking hand, strike the first string to hear it ring. Sing the syllable "sol" (pronounced "soul") to sing the note G.

TRACK 3

E note played on the open first string.

F note.

G note.

---

## Using Solfége

Throughout these lessons you'll notice the use of solfége. *Solfége* is a group of syllables used when singing notes. You may be familiar with the song "Do, Re, Mi" that starts with the words, "Doe, a deer, a female deer." That song describes seven of these syllables (do, re, mi, fa, so, la, ti). Learning these solfége syllables gives you the opportunity to sing and play simultaneously, a fundamental skill necessary to jamming, performing, and songwriting.

# Reading Quarter Notes and Rests

Along with pitch, rhythmic value is the second important part of a note. It refers to the number of beats a note receives when played. We use three types of symbols to show the rhythmic value of music played on the guitar: **Notes, rests, and slashes.**

A **quarter note** counts for one beat. The notehead for a quarter note is colored in black with a stem attached to it.

A **quarter-note rest** is a funny-looking squiggle and counts for one beat of silence. This means to stop the strings from ringing for one beat by touching them with the side of your picking hand.

*Slash notation* is an alternative to standard music notation. In standard notation chords are written using a vertical group of notes on the staff. In slash notation, notes are replaced with a chord symbol and a diagonal slash that indicates the rhythm. Slash notation notes almost always appear on the middle line of the staff, but they don't indicate pitch—only rhythm. When you see a **quarter-note slash**, strum the indicated chord once and let the strings ring as you count out one beat.

Quarter note

Quarter-note rest

Quarter-note slash

For songs with a 4/4 time signature, four quarter notes will fit in a single measure. Here's a glimpse at what these symbols will look like when you encounter them in a piece of music:

TRACK
4

Quarter notes and rests

TRACK
5

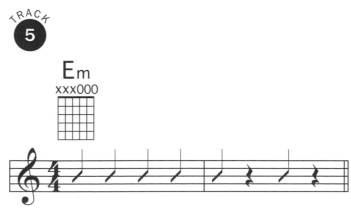

Quarter notes in slash notation

# Reading Whole Notes and Rests

A **whole note** counts for four beats. It is an empty circle on the staff without a stem.

A **whole-note rest** is a thick dash that hangs like a bat below the second line from the top of the staff. For the whole-note rest, make sure the strings have stopped ringing for four beats.

When written in slash notation, the whole note's shape changes to a diamond, but retains the same four-beat value. To play a **whole-note slash**, strike the strings and let them ring as you count out four beats.

When you see a whole note or rest in a piece of music, it usually occupies an entire measure. Here's what to look for:

| | |
|---|---|
| 𝅝 | Whole note |
| ▬ | Whole-note rest |
| ◇ | Whole-note slash |

Whole notes and rests

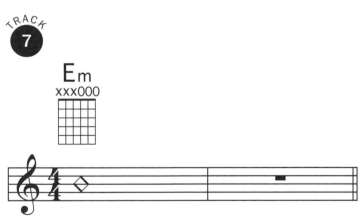

Whole notes in slash notation

# First-String Melodies

At this point, we've only covered the notes E, F, and G, but we can still use them to play some nice-sounding melodies. You don't have to play a lot of notes to make great music—all you need is a simple melody with the right chords. Be sure to count out the beats per measure as you play, either out loud or silently to yourself, just as you did with the rhythmic values in the previous examples.

## First String Thing

In "First String Thing," the guitar line consists of four whole notes, each counted for four beats, or one entire measure. In the third measure, the teacher's part changes on the third beat, but don't be surprised—you'll only be two beats into an F whole note, so continue to hold it until the beginning of measure 4.

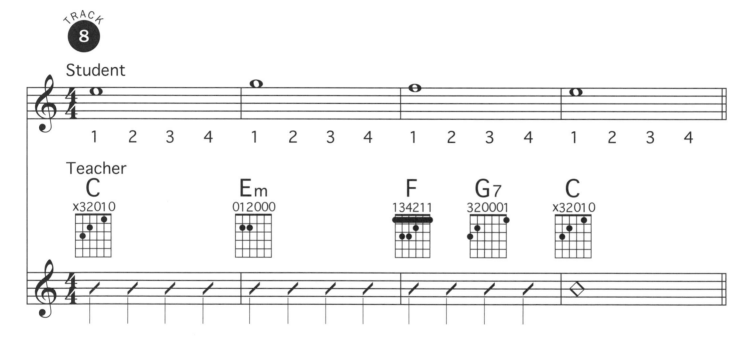

# First-String Melodies

## Quarter Note Queasiness

"Quarter Note Queasiness" has more movement than "First String Thing" because of the inclusion of quarter notes. The first and fourth measures each have a whole note, just like the previous melody. The second and third measures are where the quarter-note movement begins. Count out the beats and listen to your teacher strum the chords.

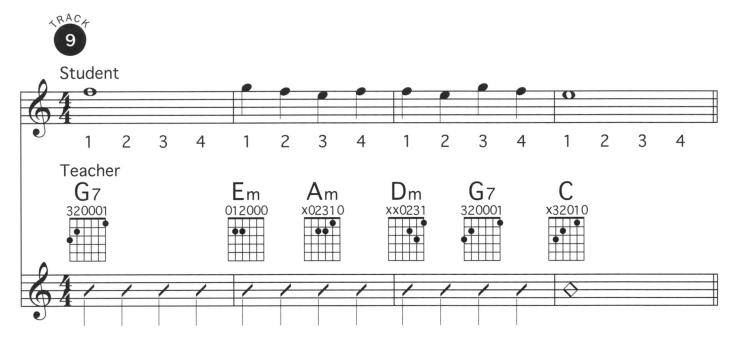

# First-String Melodies

## Roque and Roll

The third melody, "Roque and Roll," introduces quarter- and whole-note rests. When you see them, be sure to mute your strings with your picking hand. There is a quarter-note rest on beat four of measures 1 and 2. In the fourth measure, the quarter-note rest falls on beat one. The whole-note rest doesn't appear until the last measure.

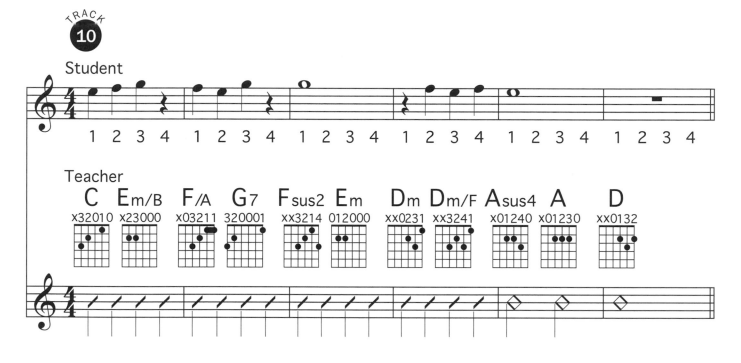

# Strumming with Downstrokes

### The Noble Man Never Runs

Downstrokes, as described at the beginning of this lesson, are often used for playing downbeats. You may have noticed that when listening to music, there are times when it's easy to nod your head, clap your hands, or tap your foot. These strong points in the music are called downbeats. When tapping your foot, the downbeat occurs when your foot meets the floor. In a time signature of 4/4, the downbeats are counted one, two, three, four, one, two, etc.

For "The Noble Man Never Runs," you'll play the chordal accompaniment while your teacher plays the melody. Since this Em chord voicing doesn't require the use of your fretting hand, use this opportunity to pay attention to the pulse. If you can, try tapping your foot and strumming at the same time.

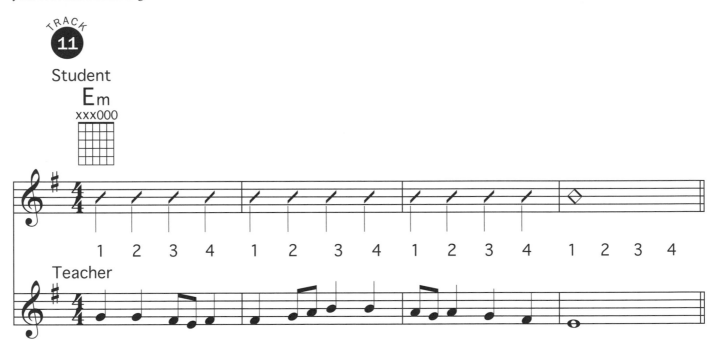

# Proper Positioning of Wrists and Shoulders

Playing guitar may not be a sport, but it's still an athletic activity. It's important to pay attention to things like posture and position, as they can affect both your comfort level and overall success in playing the instrument.

## It's All in the Wrists

Whether you play with a pick or your fingers, it's important to practice with the top side of your picking hand (opposite your palm) as flat as possible. When held properly, the top side of your wrist and forearm should form a straight line. This ensures a comfortable and relaxed position—we always want to be as relaxed as possible when we play. The benefits of this are the same for guitarists as for athletes: endurance, strength, flexibility, and speed. Keeping the fretting hand relaxed is just as important. It will improve your reach, making it easier to stretch your fingers across the fingerboard. You'll also have an easier time making any wacky shape you can dream up!

## Relax Your Shoulders

You should also do your best to keep your shoulders relaxed. When we're concentrating on something new, we often tense our shoulders without even realizing it. That is common for beginning guitarists! You can relax your shoulders simply by taking a breath and slowly exhaling. If you have a mirror at home, use it to check the position of your shoulders when you are playing the guitar. They should hang naturally, just as they do when you're standing.

Proper picking- and fretting-hand positions.

Proper shoulder position when playing guitar.

# LESSON 2

## New Chord: C

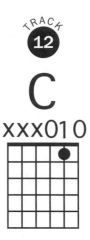

When you learned how to play the Em chord in Lesson 1, you were only strumming open strings. For our next chord, let's incorporate the fretting hand. All you will need to play the C chord pictured here is the first finger of your fretting hand. Our C chord has three notes: G on the open third string, C on the first fret of the second string, and E on the open first string. Strike the top three strings of the guitar with your pick and make sure each string is ringing clearly. Check to make sure you're using the tip of your index finger and not accidentally touching the first string. If the second string is buzzing, make sure that your finger is firmly pressing the string all the way to the fretboard and that it is close to the fret. (See "Buzzing and Pick Depth" at the end of this lesson for more information on proper fretting technique.)

This chord's full name is actually "C major," but people usually refer to major chords by their letter name alone. Major chords generally have a "happier" sound than minor chords, which have a more serious or somber tone. Compare this C chord and the Em chord from Lesson 1 to note the difference.

Fretting position for a C chord.

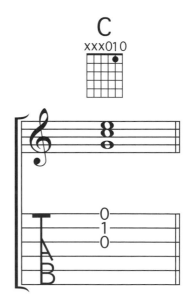

# Notes on the Second String

## B, C, and D (ti, do, re)

In Lesson 1, we learned the notes E, F, and G, all of which fell on the guitar's first string. Let's move on to the second string, where we'll learn three new notes that will expand our ability to play melodies.

## Introducing B

The middle line of the treble clef staff is where you find the note B. On the guitar, this note can be played as an open string, just like the first note we learned, E. Strike the open second string with the picking hand to hear its pitch. The solfége syllable for this note is "ti" (pronounced "tea"). Sing the syllable "ti" as you match your voice to the same pitch as the note B.

## Introducing C

On the staff, the note C sits on the third space, right above B. Using the first finger of your fretting hand, press down the second string at the first fret. With the picking hand, strike the second string to hear how it sounds. Sing the syllable, "do" (pronounced "doe") for the note C. To get a good tone, press your index finger as close as possible to the fret.

## Introducing D

The D note is located on the fourth line of the staff, right above C. Use the third finger of the fretting hand to press down the second string at the third fret. Again, with the picking hand, strike the second string to hear it ring. Sing the syllable "re" (pronounced "ray") for the note D.

B note played on the open second string.

C note.

D note.

# Reading Half Notes and Rests

A half note counts for two beats.

The notehead for a **half note** is an empty circle with a stem attached to it.

A **half-note rest** is a thick dash that sits like a hat on the middle line of the staff. When you see a half-note rest, make sure the strings have stopped ringing for a count of two.

In slash notation the half note's shape changes to a diamond with an attached stem, but keeps the same value of two beats. To play a **half-note slash**, strike the chord once and let the strings ring as you count out two beats.

In Lesson 1, we illustrated that four quarter notes or one whole note will fit into each measure of a song with a 4/4 time signature. Each half note takes up the same amount of time as two quarter notes or one half of a whole note—so two half notes fit in a 4/4 measure. Here's what they look like in a piece of music:

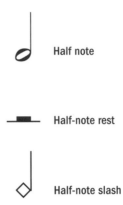

Half note

Half-note rest

Half-note slash

**Half notes and rests**

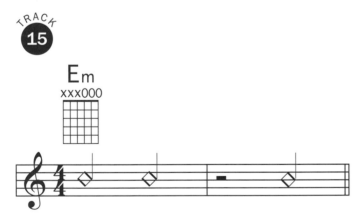

**Half notes in slash notation**

# Two Strings Are Better Than One

## Riding Horses

The first melody in this lesson, "Riding Horses," uses only the notes B, C, and D, in a rhythm mostly made up of half notes. Be ready to play quarter notes on beats three and four of the third measure—and remember, two quarter notes fill the same space as one half note.

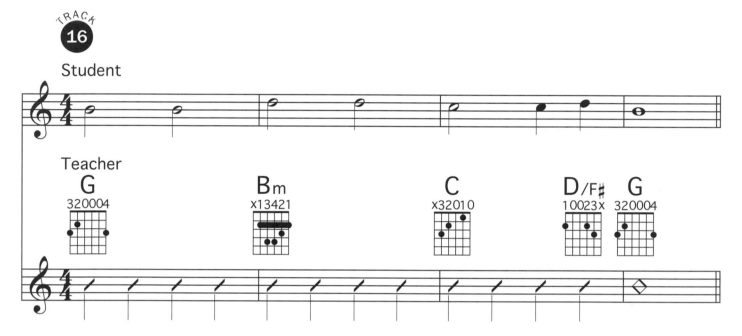

## Desert Trail

"Desert Trail" includes all of the notes we've learned so far and features a bit of extra quarter-note movement. The B note in measure 2 falls on the open second string, so use the opportunity to get into position for the high G note that follows on beat three.

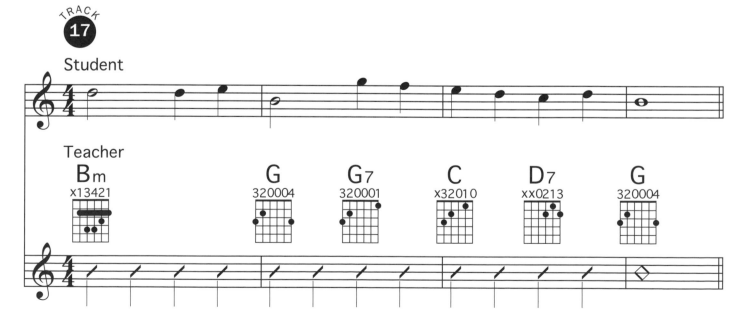

# Two Strings Are Better Than One

## Counting Encounter

The student and teacher have simultaneous half-note rests in the next melody, "Counting Encounter." Musically, rests are as important as notes. Time doesn't stop during the rests, so keep counting!

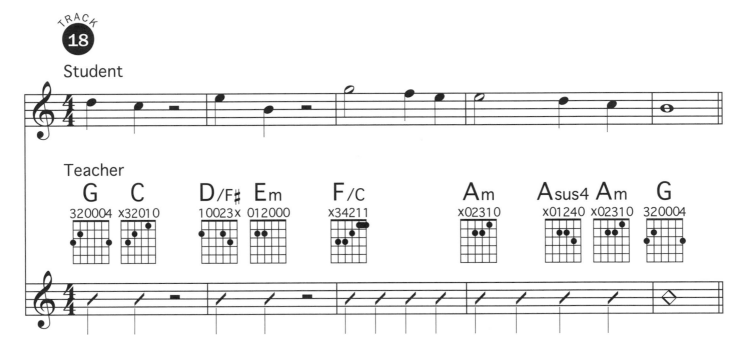

# Changing Chords While Strumming

## Eleanor's Song

You've now learned two chords, Em and C, so let's start moving between them. The pace at which you play music is called the *tempo*. Find a tempo that is slow enough for you to switch from one chord to the other while keeping a rock-steady beat. Think of your picking hand as your timekeeper as you look at "Eleanor's Song." Start by playing the Em chord while paying close attention to what your picking hand is doing. When you get to measure 2, see if you can change to a C chord while keeping your tempo steady. If you need more time, slow everything down. It's important to maintain a steady tempo and focus on making a smooth transition from chord to chord. Once you're comfortable with the movement, you can begin to speed up the tempo.

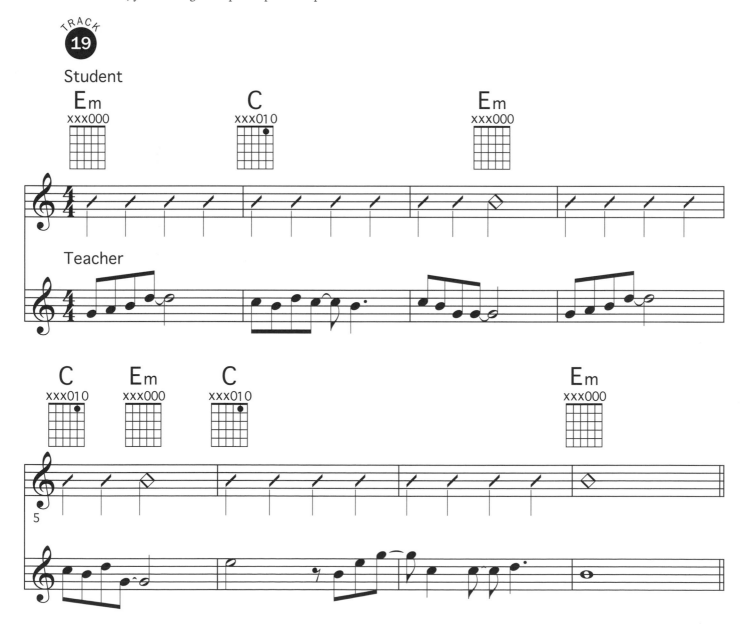

# Listening to Yourself

As you learn how to play notes and chords on the guitar, you might hear some strange sounds. Some strings may not be ringing clearly, and you might hear buzzing or harsh noises. These experiences are completely normal—but they're also undesirable, so when you hear them, you should try to correct them.

## Check Your Finger Position

If you're hearing a noise that sounds unpleasant, first make sure your fretting-hand fingers are perpendicular to the fingerboard, keeping the first joint of each finger bent so that your fingertips are making contact with the strings. It might take a while to be able to keep that first joint bent—it may want to flatten out. As your fingers gain strength and coordination, this will get easier. Bending the joint allows you to apply the right amount of pressure and helps you avoid touching and muting adjacent strings. If you're wondering how much pressure to use, remember the sage words of Goldilocks: not too much, not too little, but just right. Using too much pressure is unnecessary and too little pressure will prevent the string from ringing out.

Fret notes with your fingers perpendicular to the fingerboard.

Where you place your fingers in relation to each fret is also very important. For instance, when you want to play a G note at the third fret, you actually want to place your finger *between* the second and third frets. You'll get the purest tone if your finger is extremely close to the third fret without falling directly on top of it. Moving further (in either direction) might produce a buzzing noise, or you might muffle the note entirely. When you make a chord shape, your fingers will usually fall in slightly different places between each fret, and this is okay. If you hear unwanted string noise in your chord sound, take a look at your fingers and make small adjustments to find the best sound.

## Refine Your Picking Technique

When playing with a pick, it's best to use just a small amount of its tip. Often, beginners will "dig in too deep" and use too much of the pick. When this happens, you produce a harsh sound. Digging too deep also slows you down because your picking hand will have to work harder to strum through each string. Instead, aim to skate lightly over the strings. This technique produces a much sweeter tone and allows for faster picking and strumming.

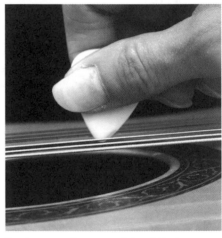
Use just a small amount of the pick's tip to avoid buzzing noises.

## Let Your Senses Be a Guide

Getting a good sound from the guitar is every guitarist's goal. Be sure to use your senses as a guide! Listen to the sounds you are making and use your eyes to guide proper finger placement. Use your sense of touch or "feel" to make sure you're using the right amount of pressure where you want it and not touching an adjacent string. Notice what you like and what you don't, and make any necessary adjustments. When you find what you like, make it your habit. In turn, what you like will help you to create your own personal sound.

# LESSON 3

## New Chord: G

Like the C chord from Lesson 2, this G chord (also called "G major") requires only one finger. This time, use the third finger of your fretting hand to play the fretted note. As always, make sure you fret the note with the tip of your finger. Our G chord has three notes: G on the open third string, B on the open second string, and G on the first string, played at the third fret. Place your pick on the third string and flick your wrist toward the floor. Listen and strive for three clear, ringing notes.

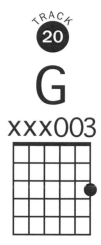

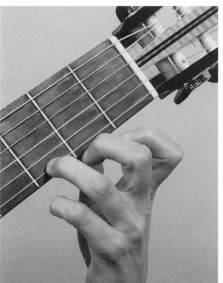

Fretting position for a G chord.

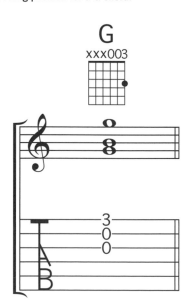

# Reading Dotted Half Notes and Rests

Most notes you'll see in a given piece of music are made up of two parts: a notehead and a stem. Occasionally, you might also see a note followed by a small dot. The dot tells you to play the note's normal duration, plus an additional *half* of that duration. For example, a half note, as we discussed in Lesson 2, is worth two beats. With a dot next to it, a half note is worth 1 ½ times its original value—three beats in total.

A **dotted half note** counts for three beats. The notehead is an empty circle with a stem attached to it, followed by a small dot.

A **dotted-half-note rest** looks like a half-note rest followed by a dot, and counts for three beats of silence.

When using slash notation, the dotted-half-note shape changes to a diamond but has the same value of three beats. To play a **dotted-half-note slash**, strike the chord once with your picking hand and let the strings ring as you count out three beats.

Dotted half notes and dotted-half-note rests take up three full beats, so a 4/4 measure (which contains four beats) is only big enough for one! The leftover beat still needs to be accounted for, so in the examples below, we've used quarter notes and rests to fill the extra time.

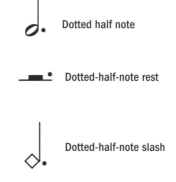

Dotted half note

Dotted-half-note rest

Dotted-half-note slash

TRACK 21

Dotted half notes and rests

**E**m
xxx000

TRACK 22

Dotted half notes in slash notation

# Learning 3/4 Time

So far, the music you have been playing has been in 4/4 time, in which there are four beats per measure and a quarter note counts for one beat. 4/4 time signatures are very common—so common, in fact, that 4/4 time is often referred to as "common time." There are different types of time signatures, however, so let's explore another: 3/4 time. In this time signature, there are only three beats per measure. To help you understand how this works and feels, clap and count along with the two exercises below:

TRACK
**23**

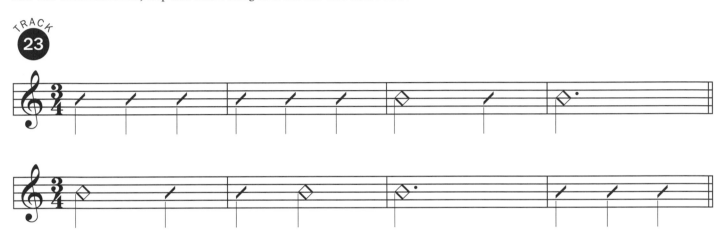

Two clapping exercises in 3/4 time

# More Melodies on Two Strings

## Unexpected Places

"Unexpected Places" begins with a large melodic leap from the lowest note we've learned so far (B) to our highest note (G). Measures 2, 3, and 4 include some smaller leaps of their own.

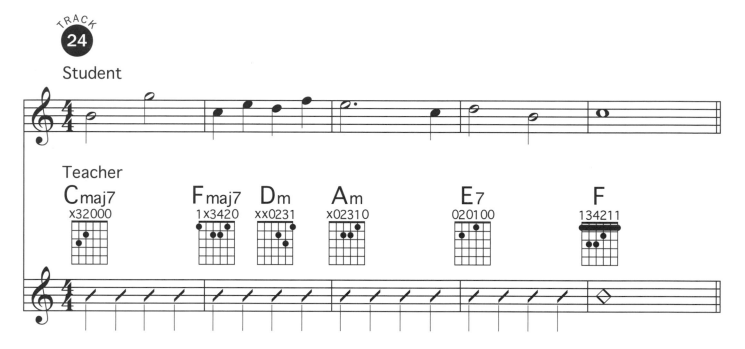

## Shark Sandwich

We test out our newest time signature, 3/4, in "Shark Sandwich." The descending melody is intended to be simple enough for you to focus on the dotted-half-note rhythm. Remember, 3/4 measures have one less beat than 4/4 measures—make sure you're only counting to three before moving on to the next measure.

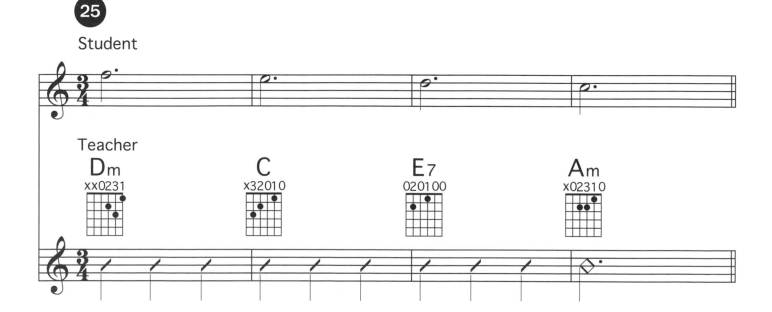

# More Melodies on Two Strings

## Langdon's Song

"Langdon's Song" is also in 3/4 time. Watch out for the quarter-note rests on beat one of measures 1, 3, and 5. Keep counting "one, two, three" and remember that in those measures, you want to keep your guitar strings silent for the first beat.

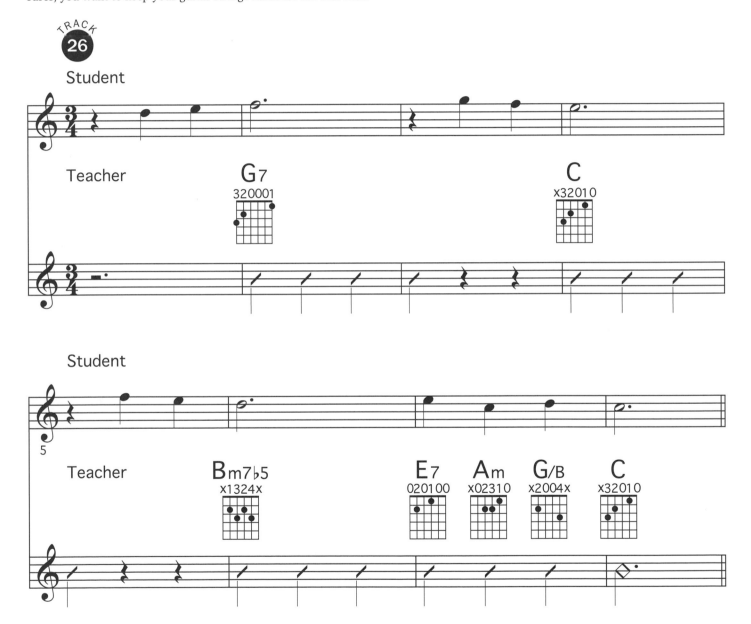

# Strumming in 3/4 Time

### Sleeveless in Seattle

With the G chord we learned at the beginning of this lesson, we now know enough chords to play a three-chord song. "Sleeveless in Seattle" combines our new G chord with Em and C from the first two lessons, and gives us another opportunity to practice what we've learned about the 3/4 time signature. Unlike the 4/4 songs we strummed along with in Lessons 1 and 2, this song features just three beats per measure. The dotted-half-note slash in measure 8 is held for three beats, just like a regular dotted half note. Keep a steady pulse and strive to play through the entire piece without stopping, even if you make a mistake.

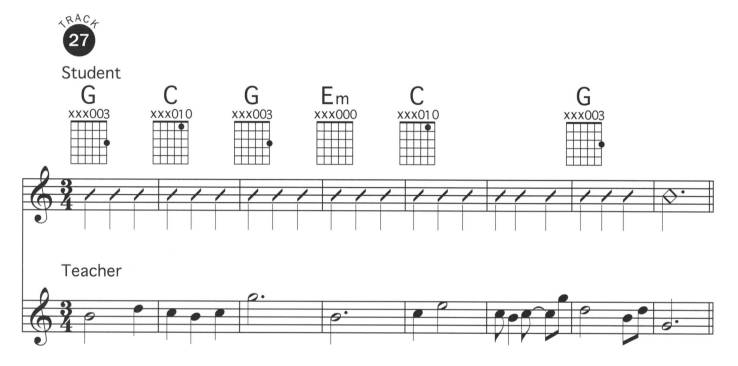

# Building Your Tonal Color Palette

*Tone* or *timbre* are words that refer to the quality of sound coming from our guitars. Different tone qualities are sometimes described as round, fat, warm, brittle, thin, or harsh. Try to think of these descriptions the way painters would think about colors in their palettes—as a painter chooses a particular color, guitarists choose a sound that they like and use it to color their playing. In this way, tone is just a means of expressing yourself, even if you're only playing a single note.

## No Such Thing as Good or Bad

To call tone "good" or "bad" takes all the fun out of it. Sometimes it's fun to talk nasally, or to growl in a voice like Cookie Monster, and it's no different on guitar. Playing with a thin or small tone can be comical, endearing, or simply a great contrast to a big, warm sound. We want to be able to use as many tones as we can dream up. It's the hallmark of a creative guitarist—and more importantly, of someone who has fun playing!

## Adjust Your Approach

To start hearing different tonal possibilities, try experimenting with different picking-hand approaches. For example, play any string on your guitar near the bridge or where the string rests in the saddle. Near the bridge, and also at the opposite end of the string near the nut, string tension is the highest, yielding a tone that is very bright and thin. This is called playing *ponticello* or *metallico*. It's the same term used for a violinist who is bowing near the violin's bridge piece. Now try playing near the bottom of the fretboard on the same string. If you have an acoustic guitar, this will be over the soundhole. The sound is at the opposite end of the spectrum: it's warm with a thick bass sound. This is called *tasto* or *sul tasto*. By playing with both ponticello and tasto tone in the same song, you create a huge difference in sound.

If you play with a pick, try changing the angle of it in relation to the string. When the pick is parallel with or "flat" against the string you get a very warm sound. If you angle the pick just a little so that it approaches the string at a diagonal, you get a more slap-like, percussive tone. Fingerstyle players can achieve similar differences in tone. Try using only the fleshiest part of your index finger to pluck the first string of the guitar—the tone should sound warm and round. To get a brighter, more pronounced tone, use the tip of the finger and fingernail.

Tone has just as much to do with the fretting hand. If you hold the string down for the full value of the note, you get a quality called *legato*. If you play notes very short with your fretting hand, it's called *staccato*. If you hold a note down and shake your finger on the string horizontally (the same direction as the string) you get what's called *vibrato*. All of these little articulations add something to your tone.

Try applying these approaches to the melodies we learned in the previous section to build your own tonal color palette!

Ponticello (top) and tasto (bottom).

Flat (left) and angled picking (right).

# LESSON 4

## New Chord: G7

TRACK
28

Our new chord for Lesson 4 is a seventh chord, and has a harmony that sets it apart from the chords we learned in Lessons 1–3. Seventh chords—also known as *dominant chords*—are characterized by a somewhat dissonant sound, a kind of tension that is typically resolved when the chord is followed by another chord that sounds pleasing. For example, tense G7 chords are often followed by C chords like the one we learned in Lesson 2 (although G7 chords can also be followed by plenty of chords *other than* C). The G7 chord shown here has three notes: G on the open third string, B on the open second string, and F on the first string, played at the first fret. As before, fret the chord, then start with your pick on the third string and flick your wrist toward the floor.

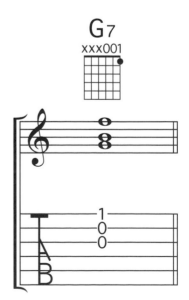

Fretting position for a G7 chord.

# Notes on the Third String

## G and A (sol, la)

Let's now look at the notes on the third string of the guitar. By the end of this section, you will have learned a total of eight notes, forming an *octave*—the distance between the two notes with the same name.

## Introducing G

The highest pitch we've covered so far was a G note on the first string. In this section, we'll learn another place to play G on the guitar, and this time, it will be the *lowest* note we've learned. This G is represented on the second line of the treble clef staff. On the guitar, this note can be played on the open third string, just as B and E can be played on the open second and first strings. Simply strike the third string with the picking hand to hear its sound. The solfége syllable for this note is "sol" (pronounced "soul").

G note played on the open third string.

## Introducing A

The note on the second space (right above G) of the staff is called A. Using the second finger on your fretting hand, press down the third string on the second fret. This is the first note you've learned that employs your second finger. With the picking hand, strike the third string to hear how it sounds. Sing the syllable, "la" (pronounced "lah") for the note A.

## Your First Octave

As we've discussed, musicians use the letters A through G to refer to different pitches. But G is by no means the highest note you can play—and nobody has ever heard of a Z note! After you play the notes A through G, the sequence repeats itself beginning on A, pitched one octave above the first A.

A note.

In the exercise below, you will play every note you've learned from the G note on the open third string all the way up to the high G on the first string. Once you get there, you will have traveled eight steps—an entire octave.

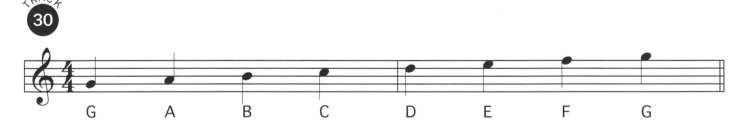

G   A   B   C   D   E   F   G

# Melodies Featuring the Third String

## Two Note Pop

In the melody, "Two Note Pop" you will play only the two new notes covered in this lesson, G and A. It starts off with a dotted half note, which you learned to play in Lesson 3. The rest of the melody is mostly quarter and half notes.

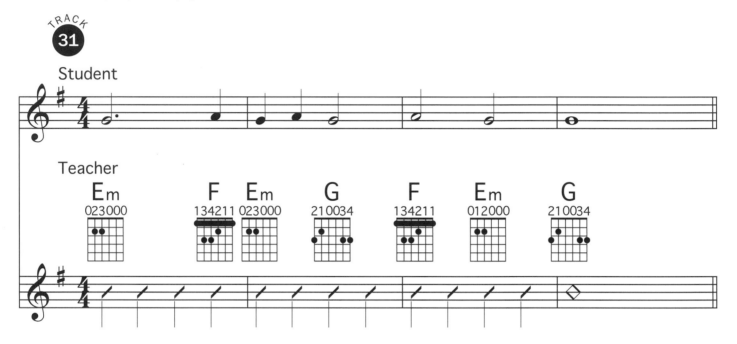

## Space Spiral

"Space Spiral" only uses notes from the second and third strings. There are a lot of half notes in this melody. Notice the similar melodic and rhythmic pattern in measures 1 and 3.

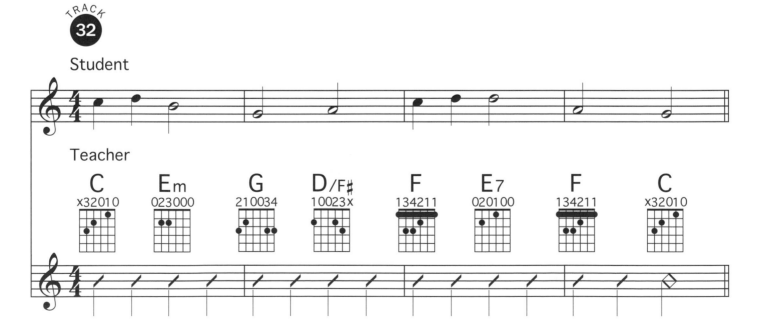

# Melodies Featuring the Third String

## Irish Green

The melody "Irish Green" features a G half note on the open third string at the beginning of each measure. It's in 3/4 time, so be sure to make the necessary adjustment in your count. Notice also how the rhythm is exactly the same in every measure, even though the pitches change slightly.

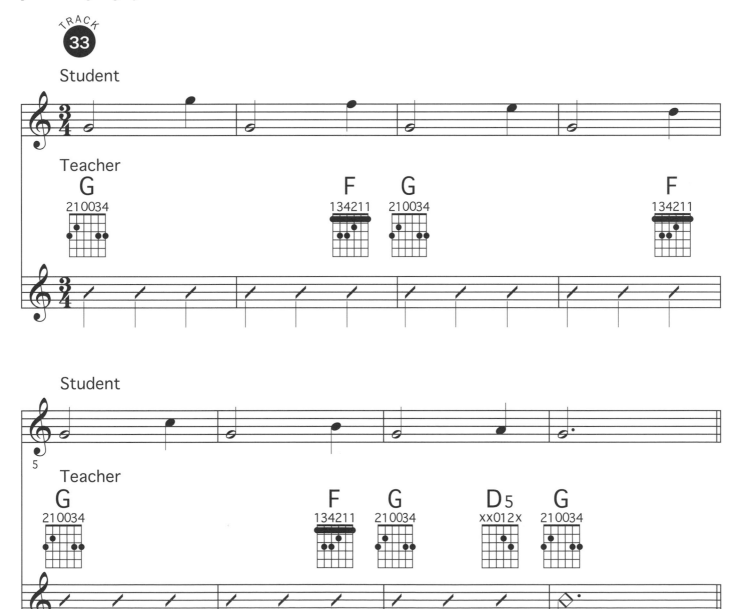

# Play a Four-Chord Song

## Hat Trick

Now that we've learned four chords, things are starting to get interesting. The next melody, "Hat Trick," uses all four of the chords we've learned so far: Em, C, G, and G7. If you're a little fuzzy on what Em and C chords look like, or if you're unsure how to count along with quarter notes, turn back to Lessons 1 and 2 for a refresher. Start slowly, keep the beat steady, and remember to keep your picking hand moving when changing between chords. As you play the chords, try to listen to the teacher's melody (while maintaining your focus on your own part). The melody features a repeating rhythmic phrase in measures 1–3, with a lot more movement in measures 5–7. In measure 7, you need to switch to a G7 chord for just one beat, so be sure to look ahead and prepare!

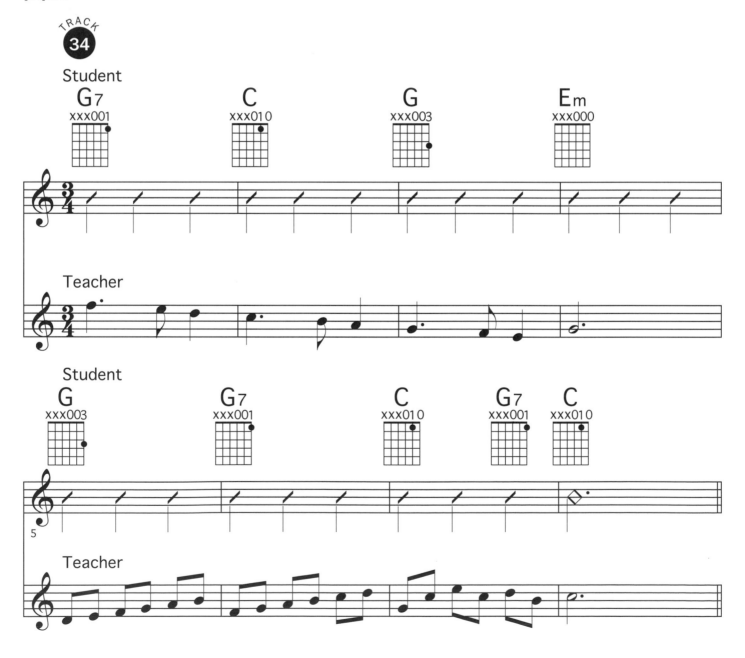

# Developing Accuracy and Coordination

At first, every new guitarist encounters some difficulty getting the picking hand to hit the intended string. It's all too easy to aim for the first string, but hit the second string by mistake. It can be very frustrating! With a little practice, however, you can improve your accuracy.

In the exercise below, you will practice playing each open string in succession. We won't be using the fretting hand at all, so take the opportunity to focus on just your picking hand. Strike only one string at a time, using a downstroke for each note. Imagine the slow and steady dribble of a basketball, and try to hit a string each time the basketball hits the floor. Play as slowly and as accurately as possible.

TRACK
35

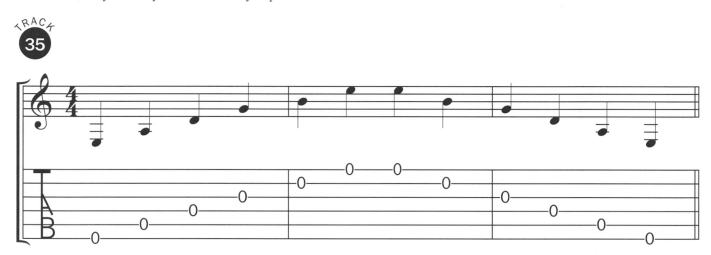

# Developing Accuracy and Coordination

## Let Your Fingers Do the Walking

The next exercise includes the fretting hand, and is designed to aid in coordination—the goal is to get both hands working together. The first four measures of this exercise require the use of the index finger of your fretting hand. Use the tip of your fretting-hand index finger to fret each note on the first fret and pick each one with a down-stroke, keeping a steady tempo. After each one, lift your index finger off of the string and use it to fret the next note. We like to call this technique "finger walking," as the finger "walks" from the sixth string, up to the first, and back again. For the next four measures, use the middle finger of your fretting hand to perform a similar walk across the fretboard. In measures 9–16, keep your fretting hand in the same position and use your ring and pinky fingers to fret notes on the third and fourth frets, respectively. As before, make sure to fret each individual note with the tip of your finger, and of course, maintain a steady tempo throughout.

TRACK
36

# LESSON 5

## New Chord: E-minor-7

In this lesson, we'll introduce a new type of chord—a "minor seventh" chord (commonly abbreviated "m7"). The sound of the Em7 chord shown here is much less dissonant than the G7 chord we covered in the last lesson. Just like the C, G, and G7 chords from Lessons 2, 3, and 4, the Em7 chord shown here requires only one finger. Place the third finger of your fretting hand on the second string at the third fret to play the chord. Use only the tip of your finger to contact the string, arching the digit enough to avoid touching the first string. This chord has three notes: G on the open third string, D on the third fret of the second string, and E on the open first string. Place your pick on the third string and flick your wrist towards the floor.

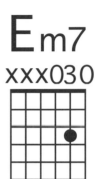

Fretting position for an E-minor-7 chord.

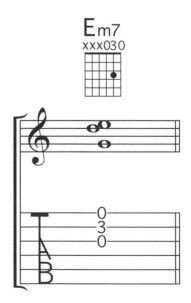

# Reading Eighth Notes and Rests

An eighth note counts for one *half* of a beat. That means you can play two eighth notes in the space of one quarter note (one beat). To understand this better, imagine again the steady basketball dribble that we described at the end of Lesson 4. If each bounce of the ball is one full beat, the first eighth note would occur when the basketball hits the floor (we'll call this the downbeat), and the second eighth note occurs when the basketball hits the player's hand (on the upbeat). One measure of eighth notes in 4/4 time would be counted like this: *one-and-two-and-three-and-four-and*. The downbeats are counted one, two, three, and four; and each upbeat is counted using the word "and."

On a staff, an **eighth note** looks like a circle colored in black with a stem attached to it that also has a small flag at the top. When there are two or more eighth notes next to each other, they are often connected or "beamed" together. See how they look in the next example.

Eighth note

An **eighth-note rest** looks something like the numeral 7 with a dot at the top end. An eighth-note rest indicates that you should stop the strings from ringing during a count of one half of a beat.

Eighth-note rest

**TRACK 38**

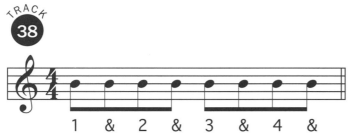

Beamed eighth notes

In slash notation, an eighth note's shape changes to a slash, but still retains its half-beat duration. Notice that the stem retains its flag. To play an **eighth-note slash**, strike the indicated chord once and let the appropriate strings ring out for half a beat. Eighth-note slashes are also often beamed together when side by side, just like the noteheads.

Eighth-note slash

**TRACK 39**

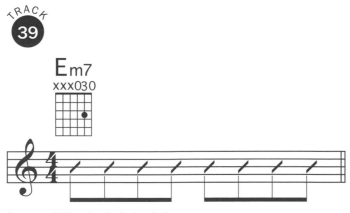

Beamed eighth notes in slash notation

# Mixing Upstrokes and Downstrokes

All of our melodies and strumming patterns so far have featured downstrokes played on downbeats (which means they've fallen on beats one, two, three, and four). With the addition of eighth notes in this chapter, you're ready to start using upstrokes. Whenever a note falls between one of the numbered beats in a measure, use an upstroke. We call these notes **upbeats**, which should make things easy enough to remember. Most guitarists obey the simple rule of thumb that downstrokes are reserved for downbeats, and upstrokes are for upbeats.

To play an upstroke, position your pick near the bottom edge of the string you'd like to play, and flick your wrist up toward the ceiling. Be mindful not to use your forearm when flicking; use only your wrist. Your wrist should move the same distance that it does when playing a downstroke. Whether you're strumming a chord or playing a single note in a melody, maintain the same shallow pick depth that you would use for a downstroke.

Try testing your rhythmic mettle in the next piece of music, a single-note melody that features E on the open first string. Measures 1, 2, and 4 require only downstrokes, but measure 3 will give you an opportunity to alternate between downstrokes and upstrokes, a technique known as **alternate picking**.

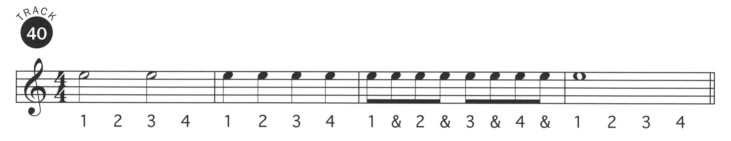

The following four measures have the exact same rhythm as the previous example, but this time, you'll be strumming a C chord. The strumming motion should use a bigger motion of your wrist than we used for single notes. Stay shallow and light with your pick.

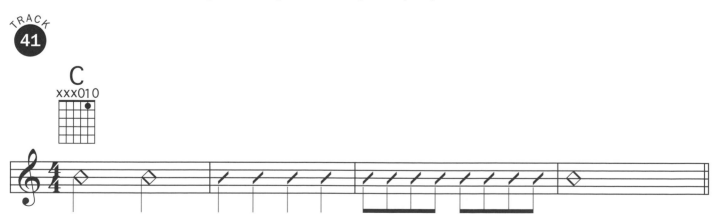

# More Three-String Melodies

## Classical Sublimation

In "Classical Sublimation," we'll review all of the notes you've learned so far. Watch out for the rest on beat three of measure 3. We give you a chance to use eighth notes on the fourth beat of measures 3 and 4.

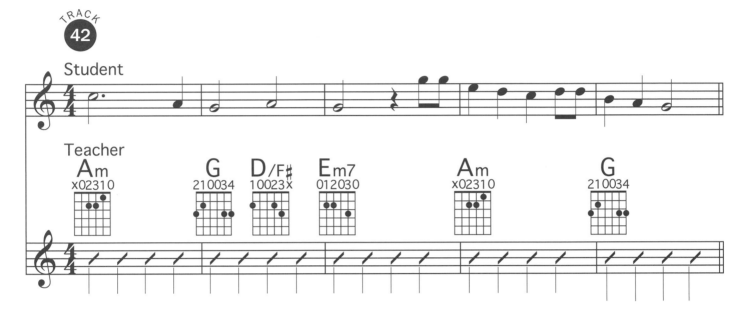

## Beginner's Patois

Next, check out "Beginner's Patois," where you won't be playing at the same time as your instructor until the very last measure. Rhythmically, you'll be "filling in the gaps" for each other. During your quarter-note rests on beats two and four, listen to your teacher's sets of eighth notes. When you play together, it should sound like four measures of unbroken eighth notes.

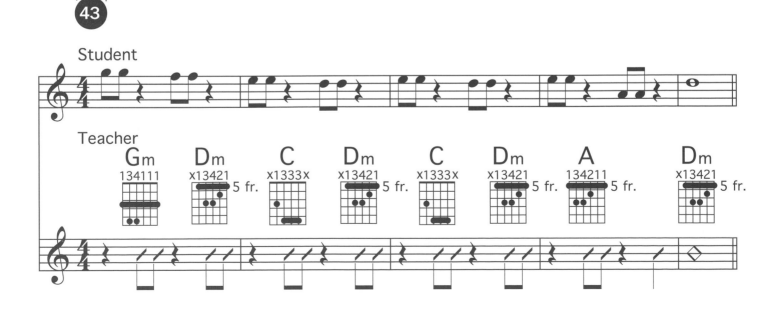

# More Three-String Melodies

## Tango Till They're Bored

Wait for two beats before entering on beat three of "Tango Till They're Bored." Notice that the melody has a repeating rhythm in measures 2, 4, and 6, although the pitches vary slightly. Each of these three measures features an eighth-note rest on beat two, which can be tricky to negotiate. Count "two" aloud before entering on the "and" of that beat.

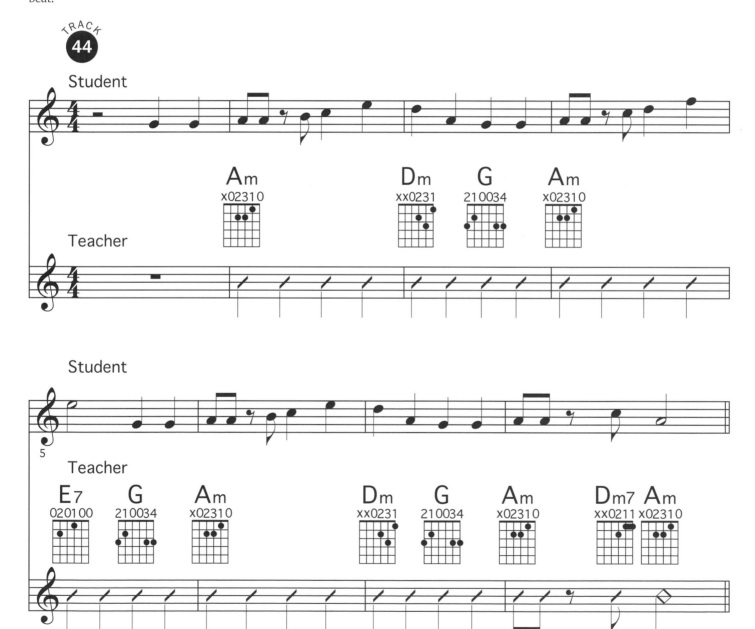

# Strumming with Quick Chord Changes

## Llama Lips

"Llama Lips" is in 3/4 time and includes our new Em7 chord. The chord changes come quickly in measures 1, 3, 5, and 7. Shift to G7 immediately after the second beat of measure 1 to catch the chord change on beat three, and be ready to change again to C for beat one of measure 2.

# Developing a Steady Tempo

Tempo is the speed at which a song is played, and it's important to keep it steady throughout a song. This is often referred to as "keeping time." Some people think of timekeeping as the drummer's job, but in fact, it's the role of every musician.

Here are some ways to help you develop the ability to keep steady time:

**Count**: Count the beats out loud as you play. Eventually, you'll be able to count to yourself.

**Clap**: Put aside your guitar and count the beats out loud while clapping the rhythm. This shifts your focus away from the pitches and toward the rhythm. It also gives you a chance to feel it in your body.

**Tap your foot**: It can be challenging to tap your foot while playing your guitar, but it gets easier with practice. Try tapping your foot once for each quarter note. If a song is in 4/4 time, you can also try tapping out just beats two and four or beats one and three, whichever feels best.

**Look ahead**: Use a rest or a held note (like a half note or a whole note) to your advantage as a chance to read ahead in the music. Reading music can be a bit like riding a bike—you don't look at where your tire is hitting the ground; you look out ahead of you to see what's coming and prepare.

**Play it slow**: When you slow down the tempo, your accuracy will improve. Play the melody once slowly and as perfectly as possible. Play it a second time at a faster tempo. Eventually the accuracy at the slower tempo will be with you at the faster speed.

**Enjoy the mistakes**: When you make mistakes, don't stop playing—it's important to keep the tempo going throughout. Treating mistakes as opportunities to discover new and interesting colors or rhythmic variations in the music is the first step to learning how to improvise. Have fun exploring!

# LESSON 6

## New Chord: A minor

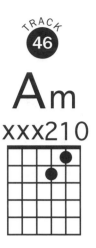

The A-minor chord (abbreviated Am) shares a similar quality with our Em from Lesson 1. All minor chords share a darker, more somber tone than their major-chord counterparts. Unlike our previous chords, you'll be using *two* fingers to play Am—the first and second fingers of your fretting hand on the second and third strings, respectively. This Am chord has three notes: A on the second fret of the third string, C on the first fret of the second string, and E on the open first string. Strum the chord with a downstroke, and listen for its sad and—depending on your mood—spooky quality.

Fretting position for an A-minor chord.

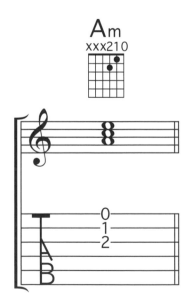

# Notes on the Fourth String

TRACK 47

### D, E, and F (re, mi, fa)

You'll now have the chance to learn three of the notes on the fourth string of the guitar: D, E, and F. As you'll remember from Lessons 1 and 2, you've already learned notes with these same letter names on the second and first strings of your guitar. The D, E, and F notes on the fourth string sound lower in pitch—each one falls one octave lower than the D, E, and F notes we covered earlier. Once you learn the notes on the fourth string below, we'll explore each octave in more depth.

### Introducing D

The fourth-string D note lives on the space just below the bottom line of the treble clef staff. On the guitar, this note can be played on the open fourth string. Simply strike the fourth string with the picking hand to hear its sound. Like the higher-octave D from Lesson 2, the solfége syllable for this note is "re" (pronounced "ray"). Try singing this syllable, and match the pitch of your voice to the sound of the open string. For the sake of comparison, play the D note from Lesson 2 (second string, third fret) and adjust your voice to the higher pitch—this is a great way to get to know the difference between the two octaves.

D note played on the open fourth string.

### Introducing E

The note that appears on the first line of the treble clef staff is called E. Using the second finger of your fretting hand, press down on the fourth string at the second fret. The wound fourth string is a bit thicker than the first three strings, which makes fretting notes just a little bit more difficult—but don't overdo it with too much pressure. When you think you've got it, strike the string with your pick to hear how the note sounds. This note falls one octave lower than the E note on the open first string, which should be quite familiar by now. Sing the syllable, "mi" (pronounced "me") to sing the note E. Again, try comparing this note to the higher-octave E that you learned in Lesson 1.

E note.

### Introducing F

The note on the first space of the treble clef staff is called F. To play this note, press down on the fourth string at the third fret with the third finger of your fretting hand. With the picking hand, strike the fourth string to hear how it sounds. Sing the syllable "fa" (pronounced "fah") for the note F, and compare this sound to the F that lives on the first string (played at the first fret).

F note.

# More Fun with Octaves

As we discussed in Lesson 4, anytime you travel up or down eight steps from any note to the note of the same name, you're moving a distance of one octave. The three exercises below show complete octave scales beginning and ending with the notes D, E, and F. Each exercise begins with the low note of the octave and travels up to the high note before descending again.

TRACK
48

Octave from D to D

Octave from E to E

Octave from F to F

# Melodies on Four Strings

## The Saddest of All Keys

"The Saddest of All Keys" is in the key of D minor (which is not *actually* the saddest of keys, despite certain famous claims to the contrary). Minor keys are often described as sounding sad or serious, but this doesn't have to mean that the tempo is slow. This melody focuses exclusively on your new notes: D, E, and F on the fourth string.

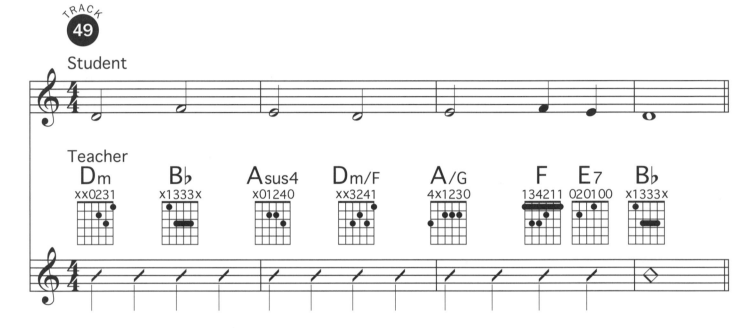

# Melodies on Four Strings

## Barbeskew

The tangy melody of "Barbeskew" incorporates all of the notes you've learned from the first four strings and features rests on beat two of measures 1, 2, 3, and 4. The rhythm may feel awkward at first, but counting will help you stay on track!

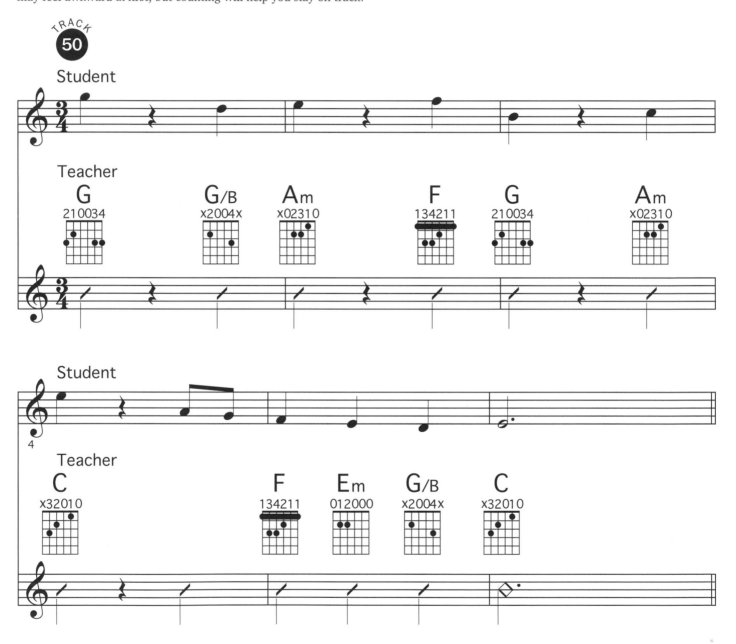

# Melodies on Four Strings

## Octogenarian Boogie

You don't have to be 80 years old to enjoy "Octogenarian Boogie," which puts your knowledge of octaves to the test. Instead of playing all the notes in between, you'll jump straight from each note to the note an octave above or below (the octaves ascend in the first half of the melody and descend in the second half). These octave leaps may require your fretting hand to stretch in some new and unfamiliar ways—the numbers next to each note indicate which finger of the fretting hand is best suited for the job (0 indicates an open string).

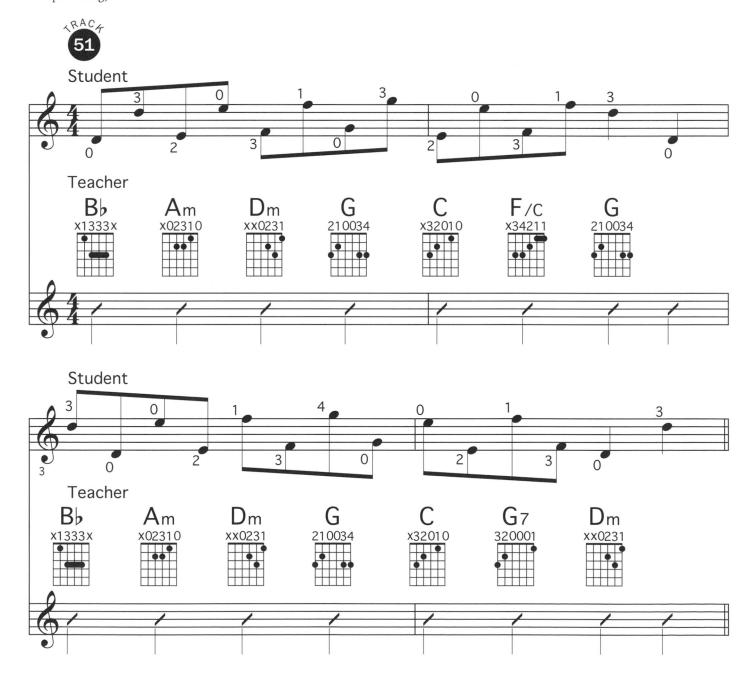

# More Practice with Quick Chord Changes

## Copycat Rhythm

As you play "Copycat Rhythm," you'll be using all of the chords you've learned thus far in this book: Em, C, G, G7, Em7, and Am. In measures 1, 2, and 6 you'll be playing two chords per measure, so remember to shift chords on beat three, and again on beat one of the following measure.

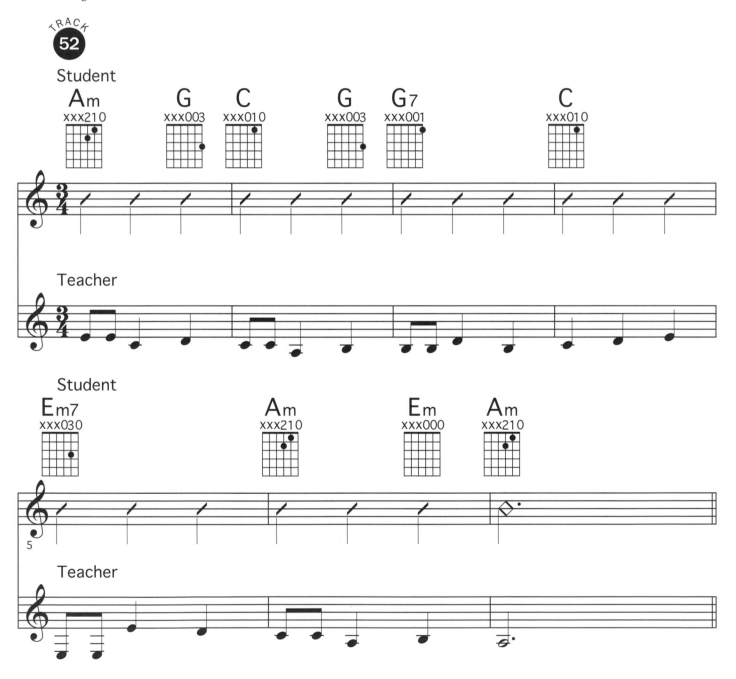

# Developing Musical Memory

Memorization is one of the most important components of a successful musical performance, and also one of the hardest to teach. Here are some good tips to keep in mind when it comes time to buckle down and memorize a tune.

## Learn by Listening

The easiest place to start is *aural learning*. This means "learning by ear" or just plain "listening." Internalize a piece of music by listening to it repeatedly. Whether you listen through the stereo in your car, your headphones on the bus, or the media player on your computer workstation, you're helping yourself memorize music. You can help this process along by actively thinking about the music as you listen: What's the next lyric? What comes after the second verse? The more you know about the parts of the song and how they fit together, the closer you are to being able to perform it!

## Focus on Small Chunks

*Micropracticing* is a term some musicians use for practicing small chunks of music through repetition. Get familiar with every note and strum of the guitar, but work on memorizing just one measure at a time. After you're comfortable with the first measure, move on to the next. When both are comfortable, link them together and practice them as a two-measure section. Use this approach for an entire song and you'll soon find that you know it inside and out!

## Distract Yourself

Although it may seem counterintuitive, finding other ways to occupy yourself while practicing is another great way to foster memorization. When you play something on guitar over and over again, it becomes muscle memory—your fingers eventually learn it so well that you don't have to think about it anymore. When learning a song, it's beneficial to sit down in private and focus only on the notes and chords. But when memorizing a song, try sitting down in front of the TV or focusing your attention on something else while you practice small pieces of the tune. When the time comes to perform the song, you'll be used to all kinds of distractions and be able to comfortably play from muscle memory.

## Connect the Dots

Lastly, we string players have access to something that many other instrumentalists do not: geometry. Paying attention to shapes and patterns created by melodies can be a great tool for memorization. Many guitarists don't read music, but can still play guitar very well because they've spent time memorizing the shapes of chords and scales. Think about the patterns you're creating when moving between the chords of a progression, or moving from one note of a melody to the next. Eventually, memorizing music and playing guitar becomes like a giant game of "connect the dots."

# LESSON 7

## New Chord: E7

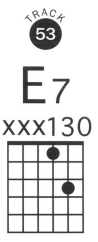

The E7 chord is a dominant chord, just like the G7 chord from Lesson 4. You'll notice that the two chords share the same crunchy dissonance (which is common to all seventh chords). As in the previous chapter, you'll be using two fingers to play E7—the first and third fingers of your fretting hand on the third and second strings, respectively. This E7 chord has three notes: G♯ on the third string, played at the first fret; D on the second string, played at third fret; and E on the open first string. Strum the chord with a down-stroke and notice the similar quality that it shares with G7.

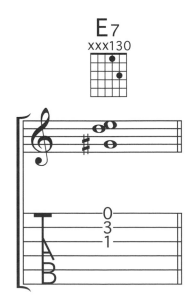

Fretting position for an E7 chord.

# Reading Eighth-Note Triplets

**Eighth-note triplets** can add rhythmic variation to melodies and chord patterns. These notes are somewhat different than the eighth notes we covered in Lesson 5. When you learned to play and count those regular eighth notes, you played two notes in the space of one quarter note, or one beat of music. Eighth-note triplets are a bit shorter—you can fit *three* of them in one beat of music, and those three notes need to be divided equally. To help you remember this, many musicians break the word "triplet" (which normally contains two syllables) into three syllables: "tri-pl-et." Each syllable represents a note of the triplet.

Eighth-note triplet

The two exercises below will give you an opportunity to test-drive the eighth-note triplet. Put aside your guitar for the first exercise and clap your hands three times per beat, making sure that each clap carries the same time value. You'll need your guitar again for the second exercise, where you will play eighth-note triplets on the first string. To start, play the first note of each triplet with a downstroke, followed by an upstroke for the second note and another downstroke for the third. You can also try playing the example with strict down-up-down-up picking (also known as **alternate picking**), although doing so will mean playing the downbeats of beats two and four with upstrokes—be careful not to get confused about where the beat is!

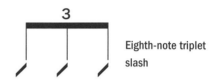

Eighth-note triplet slash

In slash notation, an eighth-note triplet retains its shape, but the noteheads are replaced by slashes. When you see an eighth-note triplet in slash notation, strum the chord using a similar downstroke-upstroke-downstroke method to the one described above.

TRACK 54

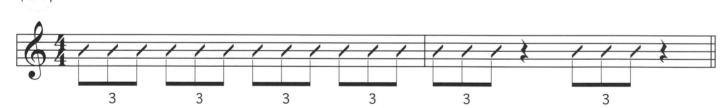

Clapping eighth-note triplets

TRACK 55

Eighth-note triplets on guitar

TRACK 56

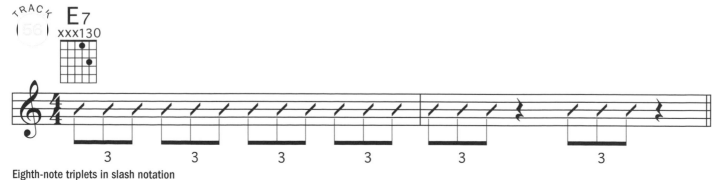

Eighth-note triplets in slash notation

# More Four-String Melodies

## A Tuplet of Triplets

Take one quick look at the melody in "A Tuplet of Triplets" and you'll notice that it's almost all triplets. When you get to the half-note rest in measure 2, continue to count beats three and four with a triplet feel—this way, when you begin playing measure 3, you won't lose the rhythm. Be on the lookout for the two quarter notes in measure 4.

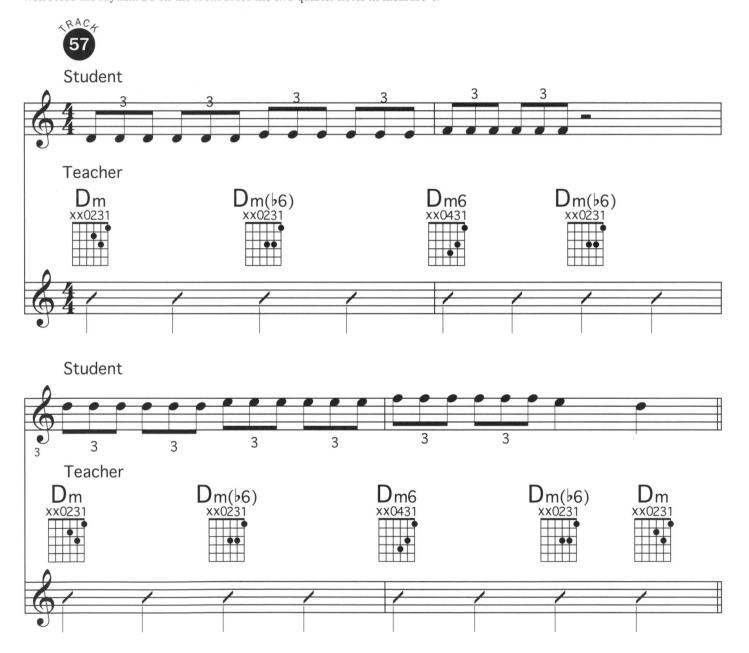

# More Four-String Melodies

## A Bucket of Biscuits

Our next melody, "A Bucket of Biscuits," is in 3/4 time. The three notes of each measure
outline the chords of the accompaniment. In musical terms, these are called **arpeggios**.
These notes happen in quick succession without a break in the pattern, so start slowly to
get comfortable with the motion.

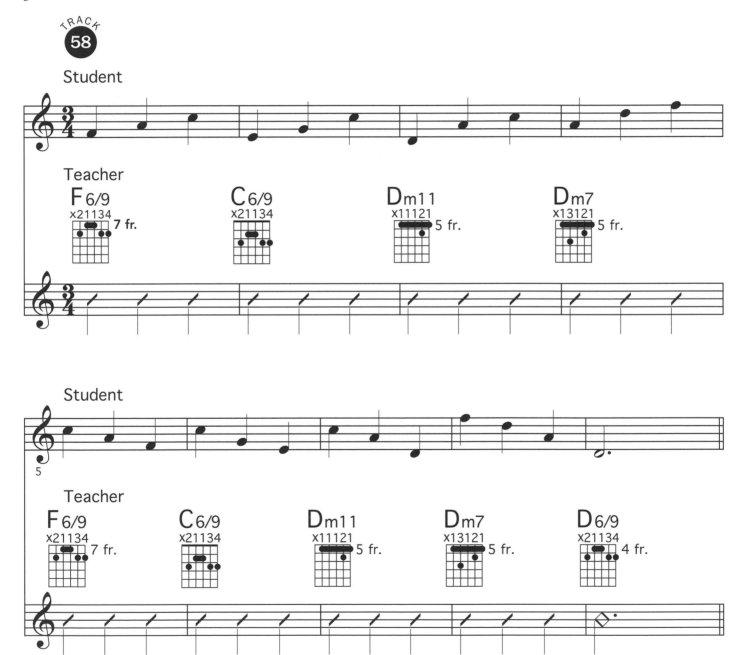

# More Four-String Melodies

## A Pocket of Piglets

We're back in 4/4 time for our next example, "A Pocket of Piglets." This melody alternates between triplets and quarter notes throughout. Try to sync your part with your teacher's quarter-note strumming pattern—the first note of each triplet and each quarter note should fall on the same beats as your teacher's quarter-note strums.

TRACK
**59**

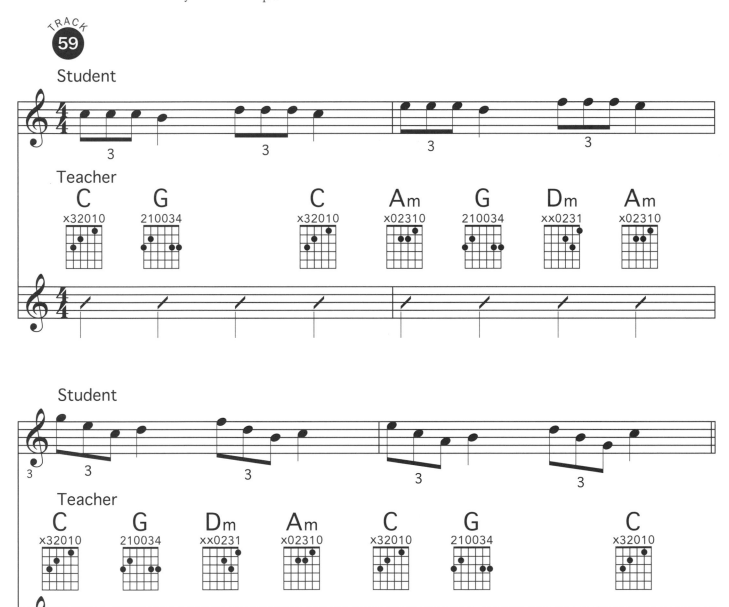

# Creating Rhythmic Variation

## More Fascinating Rhythm

In our next example, the chords are played at closer intervals as the piece progresses. "More Fascinating Rhythm" begins with a whole-note chord strum in measure 1, followed by half notes in measure 2, quarter and eighth notes in measures 3 and 4, and triplets in measure 5. The song ends as it begins, with a whole note.

# Playing Well with Others

One of the most thrilling aspects of making music is playing with other people. Every person experiences music differently—we all feel rhythm, sing melodies, and hear harmony in our own unique way. These differences make playing with others both fun and challenging. Whether the people involved are guitarists, singers, drummers, or tuba players, making music is like having a conversation. Musicians naturally cue into certain details, just like speakers in a real conversation. Here are a few things to keep in mind.

Authors Travis John Andrews and Ruth Parry share a bit of musical conversation.

## Balance and Steer Your Dynamics

At the start of any musical conversation, the first thing we often notice is how loud others are playing. In a spoken conversation, if someone is whispering, we rarely shout back at them! The same can be said of music, where, even if we're not entirely conscious of it, we tend to match the volume of the people playing around us. The musical term for this is **dynamics**, and it's sometimes written into the music itself: **piano** (notated *p* on a piece of sheet music) means you should play somewhat softer than normal; **forte** (notated *f* ) indicates that you should play a bit louder. Try to match your instructor's dynamics as you play the melodies in these lessons. As you become more aware of dynamics, try to work with other musicians to create a more dynamic group sound.

## Develop Good Rhythmic Feel

Another word often used between musicians who are playing together is **feel**, which might be described as the way rhythmic values of notes are interpreted. If two or more musicians interpret these rhythmic values differently as they play a song together, the feel is said to be "off." When you count eighth notes with your teacher, you typically count "one and two and three and four and," with an equal rhythmic value for each note. This is sometimes referred to as "straight eighths" or "straight feel." In some types of music, notably blues and jazz, it's not uncommon for players to delay the second eighth note of each beat so it sounds almost like the third note of a triplet—a feel known as "swing." Neither is technically right or wrong, but if you're playing with others, make sure you agree on which feel you're going to play before performing!

## Keep an Ear on Your Tuning

It may go without saying, but it's very important to be in tune with the musicians you are playing with. After getting ready for a rehearsal with an electronic tuner, some guitarists stop worrying about whether or not they're actually in tune with the other instruments. Any time you play with others, it's a good idea to listen carefully to your **intonation**—how accurately your instrument plays in tune—by making sure your tuning hasn't slipped (which is natural over the course of a performance). If something sounds off, don't be afraid to adjust accordingly, and give other musicians the time and patience to do the same.

# LESSON 8

## New Chord: D7

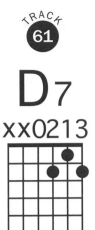

The D7 chord is another dominant-seventh chord, just like the G7 and E7 chords from Lessons 4 and 7. For the first time in this book, you'll be using four strings and three fingers to play a chord shape—the first, second, and third fingers of your fretting hand are assigned to the second, third, and first strings, respectively. We're also playing an open string, so this D7 voicing has four notes: D on the open fourth string, A on the second fret of the third string, C on the first fret of the second string, and F♯ on the second fret of the first string. Strum the chord with a downstroke, making sure to hit the fourth string.

Fretting position for a D7 chord.

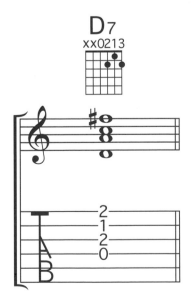

# Two Places to Play F#

The D7 chord you learned on the previous page includes a note that you may not have seen before—a note called F# (pronounced "F sharp"). The sharp symbol looks like the "pound" key on your phone, or the set of an episode of *Hollywood Squares*. Basically, any note that is followed by a sharp symbol is meant to be played one half step (or one fret) above the regular note that gives it its name—so an F# note is the note that falls one fret above F (which is sometimes called "F natural" when compared to F#). In this section we'll show you two different places to play F# on the guitar.

## Introducing F# on the First String

In Lesson 8, you learned the notes E, F, and G on the first string. An F# note on the first string occupies top line of the staff, just like the F in Lesson 8, but is accompanied by a sharp symbol. This note lives between the notes F and G, at the second fret.

F# on the first string.

## Introducing F# on Fourth String

F# can also be played one octave lower, on the fourth fret of the fourth string. In Lesson 6, you learned how to play F on the third fret of the fourth string. To play an F# on the fourth string, place your fourth finger just one fret higher. This note occupies the same place on the staff as the fourth string F, but is accompanied by a sharp symbol.

## An F# Octave

Below is a one-octave scale that ascends from the low F# note on the fourth string to the high F# note on the first string. Play through slowly and think about the letter name of each note as you play it.

F# on the fourth string.

F#    G    A    B    C    D    E    F#

# Melodies Using F♯

## Won, Too

"Won, Too" begins with an octave leap from F♯ on the first string to F♯ on the fourth string. Measures 3 and 4 have more quarter-note movement, giving you a chance to explore more of the notes you've learned thus far.

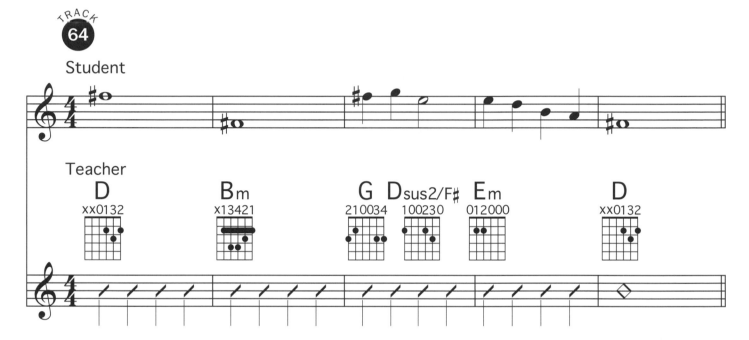

# Melodies Using F♯

## I Gotta Hole in My Foot

The melody of "I Gotta Hole in My Foot" is filled with eighth-note triplets. Remember to play these with the same three-syllable feel ("tri-pl-et") that you learned in the previous chapter. There are half-note rests on beats three and four in measures 1, 2, and 3—use those spaces to prepare for the next group of triplets. Be prepared to play both F natural and F♯!

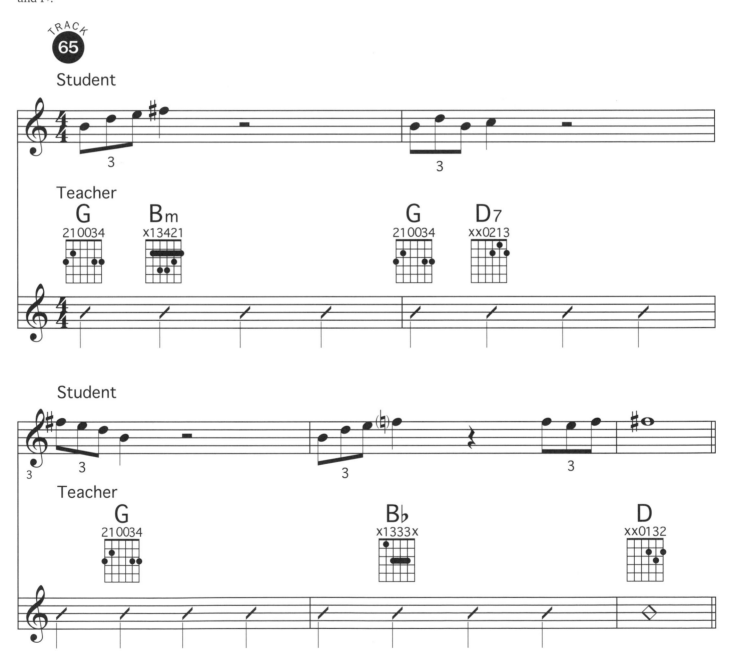

# Melodies Using F♯

## Poor, Poor, Pitiful Pluto

The next song is in 3/4 time. It also uses all of the notes you've learned except for F (although there are plenty of F♯ notes). There are no rests in this melody, so use the dotted half note in measure 2 to look ahead at measures 3 and 4.

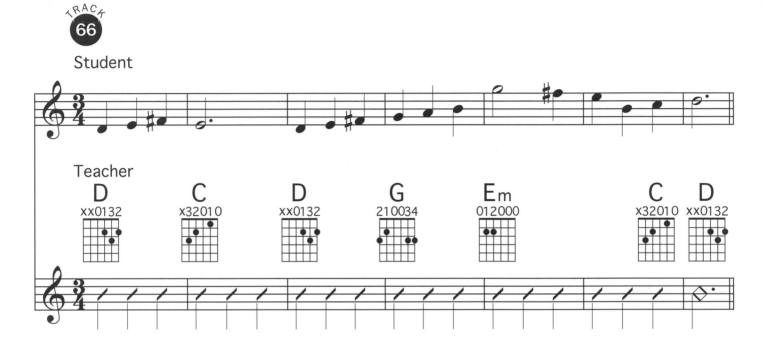

# Negotiating Rapid Chord Changes

### Two Palm Trees in Richmond

Our next example, "Two Palm Trees in Richmond," puts us back in 4/4 time and begins with our newest chord, D7. Each measure has you switching to a different chord, and each chord change occurs right after a triplet—even at slower tempos, you'll need to make those changes very quickly! Try to read ahead in the music and aim to make the transitions as smooth as possible. With the exception of Em7, this melody uses all of the chords you've learned in this book!

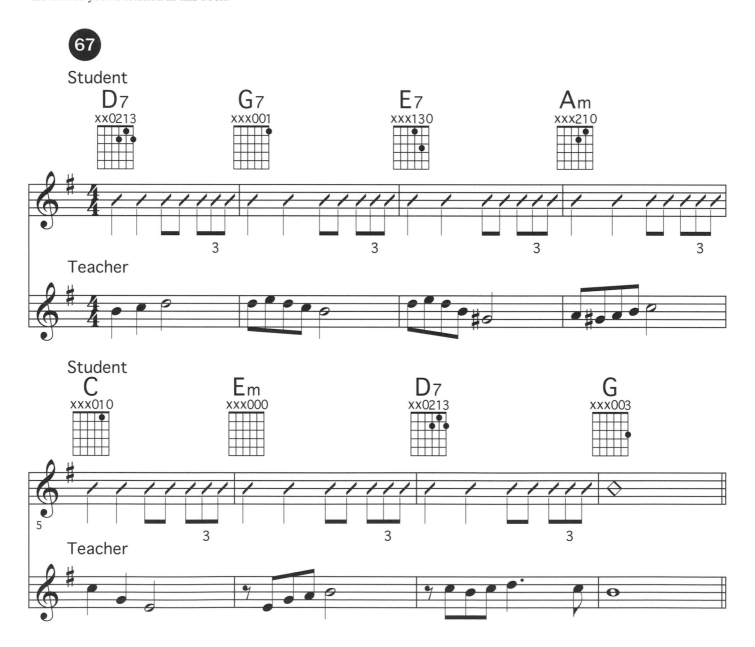

# Playing for an Audience

Take a moment to reflect on all of the information you've absorbed over the course of this book. You've learned notes on the first four strings of your guitar, plenty of chords, and quite a few rhythms. Be proud of yourself! Practicing on a regular basis is what makes us better guitar players, and if you've come this far in the book, it's obvious that you are dedicated. If you haven't already, it's a good time to begin to perform for family and friends and share the joy of music. Performing for others is an important part of playing the guitar.

## Plan Your Set

The first step is to choose what songs you would like to perform. Review all of the songs you've learned and pick the ones that sound the best and are fun to play. It's a good idea to select songs that you feel comfortable playing, because even if you are a little nervous about performing, your fingers will know exactly where to go. Once you've selected the songs, decide the order in which to play them. Musicians call this song order a "set list."

## Practice Makes Perfect

Practice your set continuously as you approach your performance date—whether it's in your living room for family members or at a recital arranged by your guitar instructor. Musicians practice a lot prior to a performance—repetition is the key to success! It's important that the songs you choose to play are "performance ready," meaning that you've practiced them enough to feel comfortable and relaxed while playing.

## Enjoy the Experience

As your performance nears, you might still feel nervous, but nerves are completely normal. Many musicians feel jumpy prior to performing. Use all of that nervous energy to have an exciting and energetic performance. It's a great opportunity to enjoy the fruits of your labors, so have fun and enjoy the experience. Once your performance is over, you'll look forward to the next one. Be sure to have an additional song waiting in the wings, just in case your audience asks you to play one more. That's called an "encore"—be prepared for it!

# ABOUT THE AUTHORS

Multi-instrumentalist **Travis John Andrews** toured nationally and internationally with several bands before completing his Bachelor of Music degree at the University of Wisconsin and his Master of Music at the San Francisco Conservatory of Music under David Tanenbaum. In 2009 he received the Conservatory's awards for Outstanding Guitarist and Outstanding Jazz Improviser. He has premiered works by Luciano Chessa and Sergio Assad, and enjoys an occasional ride on the toboggan.

Guitarist/vocalist **Ruth Parry** has performed for over 20 years in a variety of venues and recording projects. A graduate of Berklee College of Music in Boston, she has worked in a variety of musical styles and contexts, including the independent film *Jerome* by JET Productions, and has performed with Afro-Peruvian musical greats David Pinto, Marina Lavalle, and Lalo Izquierdo.

# Certificate of Completion

This certifies that

_____

has mastered *The Beginner's Guide to Guitar.*

Teacher _____

Date _____

**ACOUSTIC GUITAR**

# More Titles from String Letter Publishing

 **Roots and Blues Mandolin**
Book and CD
48 pp., $19.99
HL00696443

 **The Acoustic Guitar Fingerstyle Method**
Book and 2 CDs
80 pp., $24.95
HL00331948

 **The Acoustic Guitar Method Chord Book**
Book, 48 pp., $5.95
HL00695722

 **Rhythm Guitar Essentials**
Book and CD
72 pp., $19.99
HL00696062

 **Bluegrass Guitar Essentials**
Book and CD
72 pp., $19.95
HL00695931

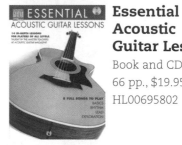 **Essential Acoustic Guitar Lessons**
Book and CD
66 pp., $19.95
HL00695802

 **Flatpicking Guitar Essentials**
Book and CD
96 pp., $19.95
HL00699174

 **Fingerstyle Guitar Essentials**
Book and CD
88 pp., $19.95
HL00699145

 **Swing Guitar Essentials**
Book and CD
80 pp., $19.95
HL00699193

 **Roots and Blues Fingerstyle Guitar**
Book and CD
96 pp., $19.95
HL00699214

 **Alternate Tunings Guitar Essentials**
Book and CD
96 pp., $19.95
HL00695557

 **Acoustic Blues Guitar Essentials**
Book and CD
72 pp., $19.95
HL00699186

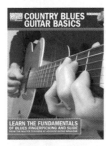 **Country Blues Guitar Basics**
Book and CD
64 pp., $19.95
HL00696222

 **Acoustic Guitar Accompaniment Basics**
Book and CD
64 pp., $14.95
HL00695430

 **Acoustic Guitar Solo Fingerstyle Basics**
Book and CD
64 pp., $14.95
HL00695597

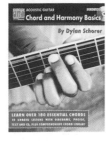 **Acoustic Guitar Chord and Harmony Basics**
Book and CD
72 pp., $16.95
HL00695611

 **Acoustic Guitar Slide Basics**
Book and CD
72 pp., $16.95
HL00695610

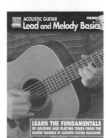 **Acoustic Guitar Lead and Melody Basics**
Book and CD
64 pp., $14.95
HL00695492

FOR MORE INFORMATION, SEE YOUR LOCAL MUSIC DEALER OR WRITE TO:

Exclusively Distributed By

 HAL•LEONARD®

7777 W. BLUEMOUND RD. P.O. BOX 13819 MILWAUKEE, WI 53213
VISIT HAL LEONARD ONLINE AT WWW.HALLEONARD.COM